Web API Security Essentials

Learn effective strategies and techniques to secure web application programming interfaces against threats and vulnerabilities

Basil U.

COPYRIGHT PAGE

About the Author

Basil is a software engineer based in Dubai, United Arab Emirate, he has worked as a Developer for over 8 years and has been building dynamic web applications, for personal and for companies world wide.

In the time past his experience has helped different kinds of companies ranging from startups to large scale enterprises. He is also vast in knowledge with CLoud Computation, Mobile Application Development, AI Integration, API Integration and Databases.

I am grateful to my family who has been a huge support to me since I started writing this book. Thanks to my wife Onyi and children for their endless support.

Content

Chapter One
Introduction to API Security
Chapter Two
Security Challenges in Web APIs
Chapter Three
Best Practices for API Authentication and Authorization
Chapter Four
Securing API Endpoints
Chapter Five
Protecting Sensitive Information
Chapter Six
Secure API Authentication and Authorization
Chapter Seven
Protecting Your API from Common Security Vulnerabilities
Chapter Eight
Monitoring and Detecting API Security Incidents
Chapter Nine
Secure API Design and Best Practices for Building Robust APIs
Chapter Ten
Managing API Versions and Ensuring Backward Compatibility
Chapter Eleven
Monitoring, Logging, and Auditing API Activity
Chapter Twelve
API security is a dynamic and ever-evolving field.

Chapter One

Introduction to API Security

Introduction

In today's digital landscape, APIs (Application Programming Interfaces) are a cornerstone of web development. They act as bridges that enable different software systems to communicate with each other. Whether you're building an e-commerce platform, a social media app, or a service for real-time data exchange, APIs allow these applications to function seamlessly.

This chapter will give you a fundamental understanding of what APIs are, why they are important, and how they facilitate modern web development. We will explore various types of APIs and walk through real-world examples to highlight their significance.

What Are APIs?

An API is a set of rules and protocols that allow different software applications to communicate with each other. APIs define the methods and data formats that applications use to request and exchange information. In essence, they act as intermediaries, allowing one piece of software to request data from another without needing to understand the inner workings of the other system.

For example, when you use a weather app on your phone, the app communicates with a weather service API to get current weather data. You don't see the complicated requests and responses behind the scenes, but the API handles it efficiently.

How APIs Power Modern Web Applications

APIs are at the heart of modern web applications. They enable developers to build feature-rich applications that rely on external services, data, and functionalities.

Some common ways APIs are used in web development include:

1. **Third-Party Integrations**: APIs allow applications to integrate with external services, like payment gateways, social media platforms, and cloud services.

2. **Data Sharing**: APIs make it easy to access and share data between different platforms, whether it's retrieving data from a database, processing it, or sending it to another service.

3. **Microservices Architecture**: In modern development, APIs enable the separation of concerns by allowing different parts of an application to communicate as independent services, facilitating scalability and flexibility.

4. **Mobile and Web Interaction**: APIs make it possible for web applications and mobile apps to interact with each other. For example, a mobile app may use an API to sync data with a central server or database.

Types of APIs

There are several types of APIs, each suited to different use cases. Below are the most commonly used API types in web development:

1. REST (Representational State Transfer) APIs
   REST is one of the most popular and widely used web API architectures. REST APIs use HTTP requests (such as GET, POST, PUT, DELETE) to interact with data. They are stateless and can handle a wide variety of tasks, from retrieving user information to updating product data.
   - Use Case: Most web applications and mobile apps use REST APIs for communication with backend servers.

2. GraphQL APIs
   GraphQL is a newer API standard developed by Facebook. Unlike REST, where multiple requests may be needed to gather data from different endpoints, GraphQL allows clients to request exactly the data they need in a single request. This

reduces the amount of data transferred and improves performance.

- Use Case: GraphQL is often used in complex applications where clients need to query multiple data sources at once.

3. **SOAP (Simple Object Access Protocol) APIs**

SOAP is a protocol for exchanging structured information in the implementation of web services. It relies on XML messages and is often used in enterprise environments, especially when high security and reliability are required.

- Use Case: SOAP APIs are commonly used in banking, payment systems, and other industries where security and standards compliance are critical.

4. **WebSocket APIs**

WebSockets provide a persistent connection between the client and the server, allowing real-time, two-way communication. This type of API is ideal for applications that require instant updates, such as live chat, notifications, or multiplayer gaming.

- ○ **Use Case**: WebSocket APIs are used for real-time communication between clients and servers.

Common API Use Cases

APIs enable a wide range of functionality and interactions in web development. Here are a few common examples:

1. **Social Media Integration**

   Many web applications allow users to log in or share content using their social media accounts. This is made possible through APIs provided by platforms like Facebook, Twitter, or Google. These APIs allow authentication, retrieving user data, and posting updates from third-party applications.

2. **Payment Processing**

   E-commerce websites and mobile apps use APIs to process payments securely. Payment gateway APIs, such as those from Stripe or PayPal, enable merchants to accept payments, handle transactions, and ensure secure data transfer between customers and the payment processors.

3. **Geolocation Services**

   Web and mobile apps often need to access location data. APIs from services like Google Maps or Mapbox provide developers with the ability to embed maps, calculate routes, and fetch location-based data such as nearby restaurants or points of interest.

4. **Data Retrieval and Aggregation**

   APIs are frequently used to fetch data from external sources or databases. This can include anything from stock market prices to weather forecasts or news updates. APIs allow developers to integrate this data into their applications, making it easy to access and display information from different sources.

Real-World Example: API in Action

Let's consider a simple e-commerce scenario. A customer visits an online store, selects a product, and proceeds to checkout. Here's how APIs play a role in each step:

1. **User Authentication**: The user logs in via an API that checks the user's credentials (username and password) against the database.

2. **Product Information**: The store's frontend application uses an API to retrieve product details, such as price, description, and availability, from the backend.

3. **Payment Processing**: When the customer enters payment information, the e-commerce app calls a payment gateway API (like Stripe) to process the transaction.

4. **Shipping Information**: Once the payment is successful, an API might be used to calculate shipping fees and offer different delivery options based on the user's location.

Chapter Two

Security Challenges in Web APIs

As the use of APIs in web and mobile applications continues to grow, securing these APIs has become more important than ever. APIs are often the gateway to an application's most valuable data, and as such, they are a prime target for cyberattacks. Whether through malicious users, data breaches, or vulnerabilities in the code, APIs present a variety of security challenges that developers must address.

In this chapter, we will explore the common security challenges that web APIs face, including various vulnerabilities, and explain how to protect your APIs from these threats. We will also dive into the **OWASP API Security Top 10**, a widely recognized list of API security risks.

Understanding the Risks: Common API Security Vulnerabilities

APIs can be vulnerable to a wide range of attacks and threats. Some of the most common risks include:

1. Lack of Authentication and Authorization

One of the most critical vulnerabilities is the lack of proper authentication and authorization mechanisms. If an API does not properly verify the identity of users (authentication) or ensure that they have permission to access specific resources (authorization), attackers can gain unauthorized access to sensitive data or perform malicious actions.

Example: A public-facing API that does not require authentication might expose sensitive customer information, making it easy for hackers to access and misuse the data.

Prevention: Use robust authentication mechanisms, such as OAuth 2.0, JWT (JSON Web Tokens), or API keys. Ensure that every API endpoint is protected and that access is granted based on the user's roles and permissions.

2. Injection Attacks

Injection attacks occur when an attacker is able to send malicious data to an API endpoint, causing it to execute unintended commands or access sensitive data. SQL injection, XML injection, and command injection are some common forms of this attack.

Example: A poorly secured API that allows user input in SQL queries can lead to an attacker injecting malicious SQL commands to manipulate the database.

Prevention: Use input validation and parameterized queries to ensure that user inputs are sanitized before interacting with the database. Avoid directly embedding user data into queries or commands.

3. Data Exposure and Insecure Data Storage

Many APIs handle sensitive data, such as user passwords, personal information, and payment details. If an API does not properly encrypt or protect this data, it can be exposed to attackers through vulnerabilities like man-in-the-middle attacks or insufficient storage encryption.

Example: An API that transmits sensitive data over HTTP instead of HTTPS could allow attackers to intercept and read the data during transmission.

Prevention: Always use HTTPS to encrypt data in transit and implement proper encryption for sensitive data stored in databases or servers. Use strong hashing algorithms (e.g., bcrypt) for passwords and avoid storing sensitive data in plain text.

4. Broken Access Control

Broken access control occurs when an API does not properly enforce restrictions on what users can and cannot do based on their permissions. Attackers may bypass access control mechanisms, allowing them to access resources or perform actions they are not authorized to.

Example: A user may gain access to another user's account or modify data they should not be able to by exploiting a weak or misconfigured access control system.

Prevention: Implement strict role-based access control (RBAC) or attribute-based access control (ABAC) to ensure that users can only access data and functionality they are authorized for. Perform regular access reviews and audits to ensure proper access control.

5. Excessive Data Exposure

When an API exposes more data than necessary, attackers can retrieve unnecessary or sensitive information that could be used for malicious purposes. APIs should only return the data that is required for a particular task.

Example: An API might return excessive details about a user, such as email addresses, phone numbers, and payment information, even if the requesting user does not need this data.

Prevention: Implement data filtering to ensure that APIs only return the minimal set of data required for the operation. Be mindful of endpoints that could unintentionally expose excessive information.

6. Misconfiguration and Default Settings

APIs that are misconfigured or rely on default settings are highly vulnerable to attacks. These misconfigurations could include weak security settings, open ports, unnecessary services, or improperly set access permissions.

Example: A newly deployed API might leave certain ports open to the internet, exposing the system to potential attacks, or it might use default credentials for sensitive services.

Prevention: Regularly review and harden the API's configuration settings. Disable unnecessary services and ports, change default credentials, and ensure that access is restricted to trusted users.

7. Insufficient Logging and Monitoring

Without proper logging and monitoring, it's difficult to detect malicious activity or security breaches in an API. An attacker can exploit an API vulnerability and leave no trace if there are no logs or alerts to track suspicious activities.

Example: An attacker might repeatedly attempt to brute-force API keys or login credentials, but without sufficient logging, the attack might go unnoticed.

Prevention: Enable logging for all API interactions and set up alerts for unusual or suspicious activity, such as a high number of failed login attempts. Ensure that logs are stored securely and are protected from tampering.

8. Denial of Service (DoS) Attacks

APIs are often targeted by denial of service (DoS) or distributed denial of service (DDoS) attacks, where the attacker floods the API with an overwhelming amount of requests, causing it to become unavailable to legitimate users.

Example: A DDoS attack could cause an API to crash or become unresponsive, impacting the availability of services for end-users.

Prevention: Implement rate limiting and throttling to limit the number of requests that can be made to an API in a given time period. Use a Web Application Firewall (WAF) or other mitigation techniques to prevent abuse.

The OWASP API Security Top 10

The **OWASP (Open Web Application Security Project)** API Security Top 10 is a comprehensive list of the most common and dangerous API security risks. This list serves as a valuable resource for developers to understand and mitigate API vulnerabilities. The following are the OWASP API Security Top 10 risks:

1. **API1:2019 – Broken Object Level Authorization (BOLA)**
   This risk arises when an API does not properly authorize user actions on individual objects,

allowing attackers to access or modify objects they shouldn't have access to.

2. **API2:2019 – Broken User Authentication**

   Weak or misconfigured authentication mechanisms allow attackers to impersonate legitimate users or gain unauthorized access to sensitive data.

3. **API3:2019 – Excessive Data Exposure**

   APIs may expose unnecessary or sensitive data to users, increasing the risk of information leakage.

4. **API4:2019 – Lack of Resources & Rate Limiting**

   APIs that don't implement rate limiting or proper resource management are vulnerable to DoS and DDoS attacks.

5. **API5:2019 – Broken Function Level Authorization**

   Insufficient authorization mechanisms allow users to access or perform actions they are not permitted to, such as accessing admin functionality.

6. **API6:2019 – Mass Assignment**

   This vulnerability occurs when an attacker can

modify object properties they shouldn't have access to by providing unexpected parameters in API requests.

7. **API7:2019 – Security Misconfiguration**

   Misconfigured API servers, databases, or components can introduce security risks if they are not properly secured.

8. **API8:2019 – Injection**

   Injection attacks (e.g., SQL injection) occur when an attacker sends malicious data that is executed by the API, often leading to unauthorized access or data loss.

9. **API9:2019 – Improper Assets Management**

   APIs that expose unprotected endpoints or insecure third-party integrations can introduce significant security risks.

10. **API10:2019 – Insufficient Logging & Monitoring**

    Without proper logging and monitoring, it's difficult to detect and respond to malicious activities or security breaches.

Chapter Three

Best Practices for API Authentication and Authorization

One of the most crucial aspects of securing APIs is ensuring that only authorized users can access sensitive data and functionality. Proper authentication and authorization are fundamental to safeguarding web applications and their data. Authentication is the process of verifying the identity of a user or system, while authorization determines what actions or resources the authenticated entity can access.

In this chapter, we will delve into best practices for API authentication and authorization, focusing on robust mechanisms, industry standards, and how to avoid common pitfalls.

Authentication: Ensuring Identity Verification

Authentication is the first line of defense in securing an API. Without verifying the identity of the client or user making the request, there is no way to know if the request is legitimate. The main goal is to verify the identity of the user or system trying to access the API. Several approaches are commonly used for authentication:

1. API Keys

An API key is a unique identifier that is passed in the API request, typically in the request header, to authenticate the user or application. API keys are simple to implement and widely used, especially for public APIs or when external third-party services are integrated.

How it works:

An API key is generated by the server when a developer registers the application. The key is sent along with every request, and the server verifies that the key is valid.

Pros:

- Simple and easy to implement.
- Good for limited access to public APIs.

Cons:

- API keys can be easily exposed in logs or through URL parameters, making them vulnerable to misuse.
- They typically lack the granularity needed for finer control over user permissions.

Best Practice:

- Never expose API keys in URLs (e.g., avoid appending them in query strings). Always pass them in HTTP headers.
- Use an API gateway or reverse proxy to prevent exposure and monitor usage.
- Implement rate limiting and logging to detect abnormal usage patterns.

2. OAuth 2.0

OAuth 2.0 is the most widely adopted authorization framework for API authentication. It allows third-party applications to access resources on behalf of a user without sharing their credentials. OAuth 2.0 is designed to work with access tokens, which grant limited access to specific API endpoints.

How it works:
OAuth 2.0 uses four main roles:

- **Resource Owner**: The entity (typically the user) who owns the data.
- **Client**: The application that wants to access the resource.
- **Authorization Server**: The server responsible for authenticating the resource owner and issuing tokens.
- **Resource Server**: The API server that hosts the protected resources.

OAuth 2.0 involves two types of tokens:

- **Access Tokens**: Temporary tokens that grant access to specific resources.
- **Refresh Tokens**: Tokens that can be used to obtain a new access token once the original one expires.

Pros:

- Highly secure and widely used in modern applications.
- Supports granular permission control using **scopes** (defining which parts of the API can be accessed).
- Can be used for both user and application-level authentication.

Cons:

- More complex to implement than API keys.
- Requires a centralized authorization server, adding complexity to the infrastructure.

Best Practice:

- Always use HTTPS to encrypt tokens in transit.
- Implement short-lived access tokens and use refresh tokens to extend the session.
- Ensure that OAuth implementations use strong, secure secrets and keys.
- Always validate the received token's signature and scope.

3. JSON Web Tokens (JWT)

JWT is a compact and self-contained way to securely transmit information between parties. It is often used as a method for stateless authentication, meaning the server does not need to store session information between requests. JWTs are commonly used in OAuth 2.0 for access tokens.

How it works:
A JWT consists of three parts:

- **Header**: Specifies the algorithm used for signing the token (e.g., HMAC SHA256, RSA).
- **Payload**: Contains the claims or user-specific information, such as user ID and roles.
- **Signature**: A cryptographic signature that verifies the authenticity of the token and ensures that it hasn't been tampered with.

Pros:

- JWTs are stateless, reducing the server's workload and need for session management.
- Tokens are compact and can be passed in HTTP headers.
- JWTs can store user roles and permissions directly within the token, streamlining authorization.

Cons:

- If a JWT is compromised, it cannot be easily revoked before it expires.
- Sensitive information in the payload should be encrypted to prevent data leakage.

Best Practice:

- Always use strong cryptographic algorithms (e.g., RS256) for signing JWTs.
- Store JWTs securely (e.g., in HTTP-only cookies or secure storage).
- Implement short expiration times for access tokens and use refresh tokens.

4. Multi-Factor Authentication (MFA)

Multi-factor authentication (MFA) is an additional layer of security that requires users to verify their identity using two or more methods: something they know (password), something they have (smartphone app or hardware token), or something they are (biometric data).

How it works:
MFA typically involves a combination of credentials, such as a username and password, followed by a one-time password (OTP) sent via SMS or an authentication app (e.g., Google Authenticator).

Pros:

- Adds a higher level of security to authentication by making it harder for attackers to impersonate legitimate users.
- Can significantly reduce the risk of unauthorized access.

Cons:

- May introduce additional complexity in the user experience.
- Requires extra infrastructure (e.g., SMS gateway or authenticator apps).

Best Practice:

- Always combine MFA with a strong primary authentication method (e.g., OAuth 2.0 or JWT).
- Use MFA for sensitive operations, such as changing passwords or accessing highly sensitive data.

Authorization: Controlling Access to Resources

Authorization ensures that authenticated users have the correct permissions to access specific resources or perform certain actions. Without proper authorization, even a legitimate user may gain unauthorized access to sensitive parts of an application. The most common methods for implementing authorization are:

1. Role-Based Access Control (RBAC)

RBAC is a widely used authorization model that assigns permissions based on a user's role. Each role corresponds to a set of permissions, and users are assigned one or more roles.

How it works:

Roles define what actions a user can perform, and permissions specify the resources that can be accessed. For example, an admin role might have full access to all API endpoints, while a regular user may only have access to certain endpoints.

Pros:

- Easy to manage and understand.
- Scalable for larger applications.

Cons:

- Can be inflexible if a user requires more fine-grained control over permissions than the roles allow.
- Managing large numbers of roles and permissions can become complex.

Best Practice:

- Keep roles and permissions simple but flexible enough to cover the required use cases.
- Regularly review and audit roles and permissions to ensure they are aligned with current requirements.

2. Attribute-Based Access Control (ABAC)

ABAC is a more granular approach to authorization. It uses attributes (e.g., user attributes, resource attributes, or environmental conditions) to determine access. This model allows more fine-tuned control over who can access resources and when.

How it works:

In ABAC, policies are defined based on attributes, such as a user's department, role, or location. A policy might say, "Only users from the marketing department can access the marketing data API."

Pros:

- Highly flexible and dynamic.
- Suitable for applications that require more complex access control.

Cons:

- Can be more complicated to implement and manage.
- Requires careful planning of attributes and policies.

Best Practice:

- Ensure that the policy engine used for ABAC is robust and can evaluate complex conditions.
- Regularly review access policies to keep them up to date.

3. Access Control Lists (ACLs)

ACLs are lists that define which users or groups have access to which resources, and what actions they can perform. Each resource (or group of resources) has an associated ACL specifying which users or roles are allowed to perform operations such as read, write, or delete.

How it works:
When a request is made, the API checks the ACL for the resource being requested and compares the user's identity to see if they have the necessary permissions.

Pros:

- Provides fine-grained control over access to resources.
- Suitable for applications with a variety of resources and user permissions.

Cons:

- ACLs can become complex to manage if there are many resources and users.
- Requires careful maintenance to avoid conflicts or misconfigurations.

Best Practice:

- Use ACLs for resources that require detailed, per-user control.
- Ensure that ACLs are regularly reviewed and updated to reflect current needs.

Chapter Four

Securing API Endpoints

While proper authentication and authorization are crucial to securing an API, securing the individual API endpoints is just as important. Vulnerabilities in the API's endpoints can expose sensitive data, allow unauthorized actions, or enable malicious users to bypass the security mechanisms in place. In this chapter, we will explore how to secure API endpoints against common vulnerabilities and ensure that only legitimate requests are processed.

We will cover strategies and best practices to protect your API from attacks such as SQL injection, cross-site scripting (XSS), cross-site request forgery (CSRF), and other threats that can compromise the security of your API.

1. SQL Injection: Protecting Against Database Manipulation

SQL injection is one of the most common and dangerous attacks against APIs that interact with a relational database. It occurs when an attacker injects malicious SQL code into a query, allowing them to manipulate the database to steal, modify, or delete data.

How it works:

SQL injection occurs when user input is incorrectly handled by the API and is used directly in SQL queries without sanitization. For example, an attacker may submit input like `' OR 1=1 --` to bypass authentication and gain unauthorized access.

How to prevent SQL Injection:

Use Prepared Statements and Parameterized Queries:

The most effective way to prevent SQL injection is to use prepared statements or parameterized queries. These techniques ensure that user input is treated as data, not executable code, and prevents it from altering the structure of the SQL query.

Example:

python

```
cursor.execute("SELECT * FROM users WHERE username = %s AND password = %s", (username, password))
```

- **Input Validation and Sanitization:**

  Always validate and sanitize user input before passing it to any database query. This includes checking for allowed characters, rejecting suspicious input (like SQL keywords), and limiting the length of input fields.

- **Limit Database Privileges:**

  Ensure that the database account used by your API has the minimum necessary privileges. For example, the account should not have DELETE or UPDATE permissions unless absolutely necessary.

Best Practice:

- Use Object-Relational Mapping (ORM) frameworks where possible, as they abstract away raw SQL queries and automatically mitigate SQL injection risks.

2. Cross-Site Scripting (XSS): Preventing Malicious Scripts

Cross-Site Scripting (XSS) is an attack where malicious scripts are injected into web pages viewed by other users. In the context of an API, this often involves injecting harmful JavaScript into responses returned to the user, allowing the attacker to steal sensitive data, session cookies, or perform actions on behalf of the victim.

How it works:

XSS typically occurs when the API includes untrusted user input in the response without proper escaping or sanitization. An attacker might submit a script such as `<script>alert('Hacked');</script>`, which is then executed in the browser of any user who views the response.

How to prevent XSS:

Sanitize and Escape Output:

Ensure that any user input included in the API response is properly escaped, so it is not treated as executable code. For example, HTML special characters like <, >, and & should be encoded into their safe equivalents.

Example:

python

```python
# Use a sanitization library or framework function
safe_content = html.escape(user_input)
```

Content Security Policy (CSP):

Implement a Content Security Policy (CSP) to restrict where scripts can be loaded from. By using CSP headers, you can prevent malicious scripts from executing even if they are injected into the page.

Example of CSP header:

plaintext

```plaintext
Content-Security-Policy: default-src 'self';
script-src 'self'; object-src 'none';
```

- Input Validation:

  Always validate input data on both the client and server sides. Reject any input that contains potentially harmful content such as `<script>` tags, JavaScript functions, or HTML elements.

Best Practice:

- Use web frameworks that automatically escape output by default, and avoid inserting untrusted data directly into HTML responses.

3. Cross-Site Request Forgery (CSRF): Preventing Unauthorized Actions

Cross-Site Request Forgery (CSRF) is an attack that tricks the user's browser into making an unintended request to a web application on which the user is authenticated. This can result in actions being performed without the user's consent, such as changing account settings, making financial transactions, or deleting data.

How it works:

In a CSRF attack, the attacker tricks the user into performing actions they didn't intend. For example, an attacker might send a link that causes a user to change their email address on a website they are logged into, without the user knowing.

How to prevent CSRF:

Use Anti-CSRF Tokens:

One of the most effective defenses against CSRF is to require an anti-CSRF token with each request. This token is a unique, unpredictable value that the client must send along with every state-changing request (like POST, PUT, or DELETE). The server then verifies that the token matches the one it generated for the user.

Example:

```
token = generate_csrf_token()
```

SameSite Cookie Attribute:

The `SameSite` cookie attribute helps mitigate CSRF attacks by restricting how cookies are sent with cross-site requests. Setting the `SameSite` attribute to `Strict` or `Lax` prevents cookies from being sent in requests initiated from third-party sites.

Example:

plaintext

```
Set-Cookie: sessionid=abc123; SameSite=Lax
```

- **Ensure Safe HTTP Methods:**

  Ensure that all sensitive operations (e.g., changing account details) are only available via HTTP methods like POST, PUT, or DELETE, rather than GET, which is susceptible to CSRF attacks.

Best Practice:

- Combine anti-CSRF tokens with the `SameSite` cookie attribute to provide multiple layers of defense against CSRF attacks.

4. Insufficient Rate Limiting: Protecting Against Abuse

Rate limiting is an essential measure to prevent abuse, such as brute-force attacks, DDoS attacks, or API scraping. Without proper rate limiting, attackers can overwhelm the API with requests, leading to service degradation or system compromise.

How it works:

Rate limiting controls the number of requests a user or client can make within a specified time window. This can be applied based on the IP address, API key, or user account. If the limit is exceeded, further requests are rejected or delayed.

How to prevent insufficient rate limiting:

- **Set Rate Limits:**

  Define a rate limit based on your application's usage patterns. For example, you could allow 100 requests per minute per user or IP address.

- **Use an API Gateway or Reverse Proxy:**

  Use an API gateway or reverse proxy (such as Nginx or Kong) to handle rate limiting and apply it consistently across your API endpoints.

- **Respond with Proper HTTP Status Codes:**

  When a rate limit is exceeded, return an HTTP `429 Too Many Requests` status code with an appropriate error message.

Best Practice:

- Implement burst handling, allowing short bursts of traffic while maintaining a steady overall rate, to avoid service disruptions for legitimate users.

5. Insecure Data Transmission: Enforcing HTTPS

APIs often handle sensitive data, and it is crucial to ensure that all communication between clients and servers is encrypted. Using plain HTTP (rather than HTTPS) exposes data to interception, tampering, and man-in-the-middle attacks.

How it works:

HTTP traffic is unencrypted and can be intercepted by attackers. HTTPS, on the other hand, encrypts all data in transit, ensuring that it cannot be read or modified by anyone other than the intended recipient.

How to prevent insecure data transmission:

- **Enforce HTTPS:**

  Always use HTTPS for all API endpoints. Redirect HTTP requests to HTTPS to ensure encryption is used.

- **Use Strong SSL/TLS Configurations:**

  Ensure that your API uses a strong SSL/TLS configuration, with up-to-date cipher suites and certificates. Disable outdated versions of TLS (like TLS 1.0 and TLS 1.1).

HSTS (HTTP Strict Transport Security):

Use the HSTS header to ensure that clients only communicate with your API over HTTPS, even if the user initially attempts to access it over HTTP.

Example of HSTS header:

plaintext

```
Strict-Transport-Security: max-age=31536000;
includeSubDomains
```

Best Practice:

- Regularly audit SSL/TLS configurations and use services like SSL Labs to test the security of your encryption.

Chapter Five

Protecting Sensitive Information

APIs often handle and store sensitive data, such as personal information, authentication tokens, payment details, and more. Ensuring the security of this data—both in transit and at rest—is essential to maintaining user privacy and safeguarding against data breaches. In this chapter, we will explore techniques to protect sensitive information, including how to securely store data, encrypt sensitive data, and safely manage API keys and credentials.

We will also cover industry standards and best practices for ensuring that sensitive data is adequately protected against unauthorized access, tampering, and theft.

1. Encryption: Ensuring Data Privacy

Encryption is one of the most effective methods for protecting sensitive data stored in your API. By encrypting data, you ensure that even if unauthorized individuals gain access to your database or storage systems, the data remains unreadable without the proper decryption keys.

How it works:
Encryption involves converting plaintext data into a coded form using an algorithm and a key. Only those with the correct decryption key can turn the encrypted data back into its original form. There are two main types of encryption used in API data protection:

- **At-Rest Encryption:**
  This refers to encrypting data while it is stored on a server or in a database. Even if someone gains unauthorized access to your storage system, the data is unusable without the encryption key.
- **In-Transit Encryption:**
  This refers to encrypting data as it travels across networks, ensuring that sensitive information is protected during transmission. HTTPS, which uses TLS/SSL, is a widely adopted method of encrypting data in transit.

How to implement encryption:

- **Use Strong Encryption Standards:**
  Use industry-standard encryption algorithms such as AES (Advanced Encryption Standard) with a 256-bit key for at-rest encryption. For in-transit encryption, always use TLS (Transport Layer Security) with the latest versions (preferably TLS 1.2 or 1.3).
- **Encrypt Database Data:**
  Ensure sensitive data, such as passwords, credit card numbers, and personal information, is encrypted before it is stored in the database. Always store only encrypted versions of sensitive data and never store plaintext passwords.
- **Key Management:**
  Proper management of encryption keys is critical. Use a secure key management system (KMS) to generate, store, and rotate encryption keys. Never hard-code keys in your codebase.

Best Practice:

- Avoid using weak or deprecated encryption algorithms (e.g., DES or RC4), and regularly update your encryption standards as new vulnerabilities are discovered.

2. Secure Password Storage: Hashing and Salting Passwords

Passwords are often the gateway to sensitive data, and poor password storage practices can leave user accounts vulnerable to brute-force attacks, credential stuffing, and data breaches. Storing passwords securely is one of the most important aspects of API security.

How it works:
Instead of storing plain-text passwords, you should store a hashed version of the password. Hashing is a one-way cryptographic operation that converts the password into a fixed-length string of characters, which cannot be reversed back into the original password. However, hashing alone is not enough—salting adds an additional layer of protection by combining the password with a random value (a salt) before hashing.

How to implement secure password storage:

- **Use Strong Hashing Algorithms:**
  Use cryptographically secure hashing algorithms like bcrypt, Argon2, or PBKDF2. These algorithms are slow by design, making brute-force attacks more difficult.

Add Salts to Hashes:
Always add a unique, random salt to each password before hashing. This ensures that even if two users have the same password, their hashed values will be different.

Example of salting and hashing with bcrypt:
python

```python
import bcrypt
salt = bcrypt.gensalt()
hashed_password =
bcrypt.hashpw(user_password.encode('utf-8'), salt)
```

-
- **Do Not Reuse Hashes:**
  Ensure that each password is hashed separately with a unique salt. Reusing the same hash or salt for multiple users can expose your system to certain types of attacks.

Best Practice:

- Regularly review and update your password hashing policies, and ensure that you are using the latest standards and algorithms for maximum security.

3. API Key and Token Management: Securing API Credentials

APIs often rely on keys or tokens to authenticate and authorize users or applications. These API credentials are critical to maintaining the security of your API, as they grant access to sensitive data and system functionalities. Proper management of API keys and tokens is essential to prevent unauthorized access and data breaches.

How it works:

API keys are typically long, random strings of characters that are sent with API requests to authenticate the requester. OAuth tokens, on the other hand, are short-lived and used to authorize specific actions on behalf of a user.

How to manage API credentials securely:

- **Do Not Hardcode Keys:**
  Never hardcode API keys, tokens, or credentials directly into your source code or configuration files. If your codebase is exposed (e.g., through version control or public repositories), the keys will be compromised. Instead, use environment variables or secure vault services to store them.
- **Use OAuth or API Gateway for Token Management:**
  For more advanced use cases, consider using OAuth for token-based authentication. OAuth allows for scoped access and ensures that tokens have limited lifespan and permissions. Implementing API gateways can help centralize and securely manage token distribution.
- **Rotate API Keys Regularly:**
  Regularly rotate your API keys and tokens to minimize the risk if they are ever exposed. Implement automated processes to update and distribute new keys, and revoke old ones.
- **Scope and Limit API Keys:**
  When issuing API keys, always apply the principle of least privilege by limiting the key's access to only the necessary resources. For example, an API key used for read-only access should not be able to modify or delete data.

Best Practice:

- Consider implementing token expiration and revocation mechanisms. If an API key or token is compromised, you should be able to quickly revoke it without disrupting service.

4. Protecting Sensitive Data in Backup and Archiving

Sensitive data often needs to be backed up for disaster recovery and archival purposes. However, improperly secured backups can be a significant vulnerability, as attackers may target backups as a way to access sensitive data without triggering alerts in the primary system.

How it works:
Data backups contain a snapshot of your database and files, and if these backups are not encrypted and stored securely, they can become a target for attackers.

How to protect data in backup and archiving:

- **Encrypt Backup Data:**
  Ensure that all backups are encrypted, both during transit and at rest. Use strong encryption algorithms to protect backup data from unauthorized access.
- **Secure Backup Storage:**
  Store backup data in a secure location with restricted access. This could be an encrypted cloud storage service, an offline storage device, or a secure data center.
- **Test Backup Security Regularly:**
  Conduct regular audits and tests of your backup

procedures to ensure that the encryption and access controls are functioning properly.

Best Practice:

- Consider using a separate backup account or server with enhanced security measures, and always verify that your backups can be restored without compromising data integrity.

5. Data Minimization: Reducing Exposure to Sensitive Information

Another effective way to secure data is to minimize the amount of sensitive information stored or processed by your API. By reducing the volume of sensitive data, you lower the chances of exposing it in the event of a breach.

How it works:
Data minimization involves only collecting and storing the data that is necessary for the application to function. For example, rather than storing a full credit card number, you might store just the last four digits and use tokenization for the rest.

How to implement data minimization:

- Limit Data Collection:
  Only collect the minimum amount of data needed to provide the service. Avoid storing sensitive information unless absolutely necessary, and delete any data that is no longer needed.
- Use Tokenization or Redaction:
  Tokenization replaces sensitive data with non-sensitive equivalents (tokens), making it

impossible for attackers to access the original data. Redacting or masking sensitive information in logs and responses also helps limit exposure.

Best Practice:

- Implement data retention policies and periodically review the data you store, ensuring that outdated or unnecessary sensitive data is securely deleted.

Chapter Six

Secure API Authentication and Authorization

Authentication and authorization are core components of API security. While authentication ensures that the user or system interacting with your API is who they claim to be, authorization determines what actions that authenticated entity is allowed to perform. Implementing robust and secure mechanisms for both authentication and authorization is essential for protecting sensitive resources, preventing unauthorized access, and ensuring that only legitimate users can perform specific actions.

In this chapter, we will explore the various authentication and authorization strategies used in API security, including methods like OAuth, JWT (JSON Web Tokens), API keys, and role-based access control (RBAC). We will also discuss how to avoid common pitfalls and implement best practices for secure user and system identity management.

1. Understanding Authentication and Authorization

Before diving into the specific technologies and practices, let's first define authentication and authorization in the context of APIs:

- **Authentication** is the process of verifying the identity of a user or system. It typically involves checking credentials such as usernames, passwords, API keys, or tokens to confirm that the requester is legitimate.

- **Authorization** comes after authentication and determines what actions the authenticated entity is permitted to perform. This might involve checking the user's roles or permissions to decide if they have access to a specific resource or operation.

2. Authentication Methods for APIs

There are several authentication methods commonly used in APIs to ensure secure access. Each method has its advantages and is suitable for different scenarios. Let's explore the most common authentication mechanisms:

API Keys

API keys are a simple form of authentication where an API key, a unique string, is provided with each API request. The server checks the API key to identify the user or application making the request. While easy to implement, API keys are generally not sufficient for securing highly sensitive data because they lack robust validation, user verification, and fine-grained access control.

How to implement API Key Authentication:

- Generate a unique API key for each user or system.
- Send the API key in the HTTP headers (e.g., `Authorization: ApiKey <your-api-key>`) or as a query parameter.
- Check the API key on the server against your database or a key management service to validate the request.

Best Practice:

- Ensure API keys are not exposed in public repositories or client-side code.
- Use SSL/TLS to protect API key transmission.

Basic Authentication

Basic Authentication involves sending a username and password with each request. This method is typically combined with HTTPS to ensure that the credentials are encrypted during transit. However, basic authentication is not recommended for high-security applications because it involves sending plaintext credentials with each request (even if the transmission is encrypted).

How to implement Basic Authentication:

- The client sends the username and password in the `Authorization` header (e.g., `Authorization: Basic base64encoded(username:password)`).
- The server decodes and verifies the credentials.

Best Practice:

- Avoid using Basic Authentication over HTTP; always use HTTPS to encrypt the credentials.

OAuth 2.0

OAuth 2.0 is one of the most widely used authentication protocols, especially for allowing third-party applications to access user data without exposing credentials. OAuth uses tokens to authenticate users and authorize actions, providing more fine-grained control over what the authenticated entity can do.

OAuth 2.0 works through the exchange of an authorization code for an access token. Access tokens are used to access the user's resources, and refresh tokens can be used to obtain new access tokens without requiring the user to reauthenticate.

How to implement OAuth 2.0:

1. **Authorization Request:**
   The client application requests authorization from the user.
2. **Authorization Code Exchange:**
   The authorization server returns an authorization code to the client after the user consents.
3. **Token Exchange:**
   The client exchanges the authorization code for an access token and refresh token.
4. **Access API with Token:**
   The client sends the access token with each API request (typically in the `Authorization` header).

Best Practice:

- Always use HTTPS for OAuth to protect token exchanges.
- Implement token expiration and revocation mechanisms to prevent unauthorized access when tokens are compromised.

JWT (JSON Web Tokens)

JWT is a compact, URL-safe method for transmitting information between parties as a JSON object. It is often used in combination with OAuth 2.0 to transmit access tokens. The advantage of JWT is that it can carry user claims (like user roles, permissions, or session information) and is stateless, meaning the server does not need to store session data.

How to implement JWT Authentication:

1. **Authentication:**
   The user logs in and the server generates a JWT token containing claims about the user (e.g., user ID, roles).
2. **Token Issuance:**
   The server returns the JWT to the client.
3. **Subsequent Requests:**
   The client sends the JWT in the `Authorization` header (e.g., `Authorization: Bearer <JWT-token>`).
4. **Verification:**
   The server verifies the token's authenticity using a secret or public key and grants or denies access based on the claims in the token.

Best Practice:

- Use short-lived JWT tokens and refresh them as needed to limit the impact of token compromise.
- Store the secret key securely and avoid exposing it in the code.

3. Authorization: Defining Permissions and Access Control

Once a user is authenticated, the next step is to determine what resources and actions they are allowed to access. There are several access control mechanisms available to enforce authorization:

Role-Based Access Control (RBAC)

RBAC is one of the most common ways to manage access control in APIs. It assigns roles to users, and each role has specific permissions associated with it. For example, an "admin" might have full access to all resources, while a "viewer" role may only have read access.

How to implement RBAC:

- Define roles (e.g., admin, editor, viewer).
- Assign users to one or more roles.
- Each role has associated permissions (e.g., read, write, delete).

Best Practice:

- Apply the principle of least privilege—users should only have the minimum permissions necessary to perform their tasks.

Attribute-Based Access Control (ABAC)

ABAC is a more dynamic approach to access control. It evaluates multiple attributes (e.g., user role, time of day, resource type) to determine if access should be granted. ABAC is more flexible than RBAC and can accommodate complex access control requirements.

How to implement ABAC:

- Define attributes for users, resources, and actions.
- Implement logic that checks if the combination of these attributes allows the user to perform the action.

Best Practice:

- ABAC can be complex to manage, so it's best to clearly document all attributes and policies used to determine access.

4. Combining Authentication and Authorization

To secure your API, it's essential to combine both strong authentication and robust authorization:

- **Authenticate first**: Verify that the user or system making the request is legitimate (e.g., using OAuth, JWT).
- **Authorize second**: Once authenticated, verify the user's access to the specific resource or action (e.g., using RBAC or ABAC).

Best Practice:

- Use fine-grained access control to restrict users based on roles, permissions, and attributes. For sensitive operations, implement additional layers of authentication, such as multi-factor authentication (MFA).

5. Common Pitfalls and How to Avoid Them

1. **Weak Password Storage:**
   Avoid storing passwords in plaintext. Use strong hashing algorithms (e.g., bcrypt) with salts.
2. **Hardcoding Credentials:**
   Never hardcode API keys, credentials, or tokens in your source code. Use secure vaults or environment variables.
3. **Lack of Token Expiration:**
   Tokens should have an expiration time. Long-lived tokens increase the risk of compromise. Implement token rotation to improve security.
4. **Excessive Permissions:**
   Ensure that users only have the permissions necessary for their tasks. Use RBAC to enforce this principle.

5. **Not Implementing Multi-Factor Authentication (MFA):**
   For critical actions, enforce MFA to add an additional layer of security.

Chapter Seven

Protecting Your API from Common Security Vulnerabilities

APIs are the backbone of modern web and mobile applications, but they are also frequent targets for cyberattacks. As an API developer, it's crucial to understand the common security vulnerabilities that can expose your API to risks. These vulnerabilities can lead to data breaches, unauthorized access, and other critical security issues. In this chapter, we'll explore some of the most common vulnerabilities and provide practical guidance on how to protect your API from them.

We'll focus on security flaws such as SQL Injection, Cross-Site Scripting (XSS), Cross-Site Request Forgery (CSRF), insecure deserialization, and improper access control, and provide strategies to mitigate these risks. By the end of this chapter, you'll have a better understanding of how to safeguard your API from common threats and how to implement best practices for API security.

1. Understanding Common API Vulnerabilities

APIs, like any software, are vulnerable to a variety of attacks. While there are many potential security threats, some are more common and dangerous than others. Understanding these vulnerabilities and how to protect against them is crucial to securing your API.

Here are some of the most prevalent API security vulnerabilities:

SQL Injection (SQLi)

SQL Injection occurs when an attacker manipulates an SQL query by inserting or altering SQL statements within an API request. If the API does not properly validate or sanitize input, this can allow attackers to execute arbitrary SQL commands, potentially compromising the database, accessing sensitive data, or modifying the database structure.

How to mitigate SQL Injection:

- **Use Prepared Statements:** Ensure all database queries are written using prepared statements or parameterized queries, which separate the data from the query structure, preventing manipulation.

- **Input Validation:** Always validate user inputs. Ensure that data entered into forms or API requests meets expected formats (e.g., alphanumeric, no special characters for usernames).

- **Escape Input:** For cases where direct queries are necessary, use an escaping mechanism to sanitize input before embedding it into the query.

Best Practice:

- Employ an ORM (Object-Relational Mapping) tool for database queries, as they often provide automatic protection against SQL Injection.

Cross-Site Scripting (XSS)

XSS occurs when an attacker injects malicious scripts into web pages that are viewed by other users. If your API returns data that is not properly sanitized, malicious scripts could be executed in a user's browser, leading to data theft, session hijacking, or other malicious actions.

How to mitigate XSS:

- **Escape Output:** Ensure that any data returned from the API is properly sanitized or escaped, especially when it will be rendered in the browser.

- **Use a Content Security Policy (CSP):** Implement CSP headers to restrict which scripts can run on your website, reducing the risk of malicious content being executed.

- **Validate Input and Output:** Always validate both input (before it's stored) and output (before it's displayed) to prevent harmful code from being processed or returned.

Best Practice:

- If your API handles HTML or JavaScript, be sure to use a library or framework that automatically escapes dangerous characters.

Cross-Site Request Forgery (CSRF)

CSRF attacks occur when an attacker tricks a user into performing actions without their consent or knowledge. These attacks are especially dangerous for state-changing actions, like transferring money or changing a user's password. This is typically done by embedding a malicious request into a webpage, which is automatically executed when the user unknowingly interacts with it.

How to mitigate CSRF:

- **Use Anti-CSRF Tokens:** Include unique, unpredictable tokens in all state-changing requests. This token should be checked by the API to confirm that the request was made intentionally by the authenticated user.

- **SameSite Cookies:** Set the SameSite attribute for cookies to Strict or Lax to prevent cookies from being sent in cross-origin requests.

- Use the `Origin` or `Referer` Header: Check the `Origin` or `Referer` header in HTTP requests to ensure the request is coming from a trusted domain.

Best Practice:

- Always require the use of CSRF tokens in forms and API requests that perform state-changing operations.

Insecure Deserialization

Insecure deserialization occurs when an attacker exploits an API's deserialization process to inject malicious data. This can lead to remote code execution, data manipulation, or denial of service.

How to mitigate Insecure Deserialization:

- Avoid Deserialization of Untrusted Data: Never deserialize data from untrusted or unauthenticated sources, especially user-controlled data.

- **Use Safe Serialization Formats:** Prefer using safer serialization formats such as JSON instead of formats like XML, which are vulnerable to certain deserialization attacks.

- **Validate and Sanitize Data:** Ensure that data is validated and sanitized before it is deserialized.

Best Practice:

- If deserialization is necessary, implement strict data validation and avoid using weak serialization libraries that allow for manipulation.

2. Implementing Proper Access Control

Access control determines which users or systems are allowed to access certain resources or perform specific actions. Poorly implemented access control mechanisms can expose sensitive data and lead to unauthorized access. There are several common pitfalls to be aware of when designing API access control.

Broken Access Control

Broken access control occurs when an attacker is able to bypass or manipulate the authorization mechanisms that are intended to restrict access to sensitive resources. This could involve exploiting poorly defined roles, permissions, or URL access restrictions.

How to mitigate Broken Access Control:

- **Enforce Principle of Least Privilege:** Only grant users or systems the minimal permissions needed to perform their tasks.

- **Validate Access for Every Request:** Never assume that users or systems with specific roles automatically have access to all resources. Validate their access for each API request.

- **Use Role-Based Access Control (RBAC):** RBAC helps manage access permissions based on the user's role, limiting the scope of access.

Best Practice:

- Regularly audit and test your API's access control mechanisms to identify and patch any vulnerabilities.

3. Mitigating API Abuse and Rate Limiting

APIs are often vulnerable to abuse, either by malicious users or systems making an overwhelming number of requests, potentially leading to service degradation or downtime.

Denial of Service (DoS) Attacks

DoS attacks occur when an attacker floods an API with requests in an attempt to exhaust server resources, leading to downtime or degradation of services.

How to mitigate DoS attacks:

- **Rate Limiting:** Implement rate limiting to restrict the number of requests a client can make within a specific time period. For example, you can allow a maximum of 100 requests per minute.
- **API Throttling:** Throttle requests when a client exceeds the allowed rate limit to prevent abuse.
- **IP Blocking:** Block or limit access to known malicious IP addresses.

Best Practice:

- Use a Web Application Firewall (WAF) to detect and block malicious traffic before it reaches your API.

API Key Abuse

API keys are often used to authenticate and authorize users, but they can be easily abused if they fall into the wrong hands. If an API key is compromised, it can lead to unauthorized access to sensitive resources.

How to mitigate API Key Abuse:

- **Rotate API Keys:** Regularly rotate API keys to minimize the impact of a key being compromised.
- **IP Whitelisting:** Restrict the use of API keys to specific IP addresses to prevent unauthorized use.
- **Monitor API Usage:** Implement logging and monitoring to track API usage and identify suspicious patterns of activity.

Best Practice:

- Use short-lived tokens (e.g., JWT) for more secure and flexible authentication instead of relying solely on long-lived API keys.

4. Secure API Logging and Monitoring

Logging and monitoring are essential components of API security. By keeping track of API requests, responses, and errors, you can detect potential security incidents and respond quickly.

How to Implement Secure Logging:

- **Log All Access Attempts:** Record all access attempts, including successful and failed authentication and authorization attempts.

- **Sanitize Logs:** Do not store sensitive information like passwords, tokens, or API keys in logs.

- **Monitor for Suspicious Activity:** Regularly review logs for patterns of suspicious behavior, such as abnormal usage spikes or unauthorized access attempts.

Best Practice:

- Set up alerts for unusual patterns of behavior that may indicate an attack or vulnerability.

Chapter Eight

Monitoring and Detecting API Security Incidents

API security doesn't end once you've implemented protective measures such as access control, encryption, and authentication mechanisms. Continuous monitoring and incident detection are essential components of a robust API security strategy. APIs are dynamic, and new vulnerabilities may emerge over time. Therefore, you must be able to detect potential threats and respond swiftly to mitigate the risks of a security breach.

In this chapter, we'll explore the importance of monitoring your APIs for security incidents, the tools and techniques available to track API activity, and best practices for detecting and responding to incidents. By the end of this chapter, you'll understand how to implement a monitoring and detection strategy that can help safeguard your API from emerging threats and attacks.

1. The Importance of API Security Monitoring

API security monitoring is critical to maintaining a secure environment, as it helps you identify and respond to potential threats before they result in significant damage. Monitoring allows you to:

- **Identify Suspicious Activity:** Monitor for signs of unauthorized access, unusual traffic patterns, and abnormal user behavior.

- **Detect Vulnerabilities:** Quickly discover security flaws and vulnerabilities that could be exploited by attackers.

- **Ensure Compliance:** If your API handles sensitive or regulated data, regular monitoring helps ensure compliance with industry standards like GDPR, HIPAA, or PCI-DSS.

- **Improve Response Times:** Detecting issues early enables you to respond promptly and minimize the impact of security incidents.

Regular monitoring helps you stay ahead of cyber threats and reduces the chances of a successful attack on your API.

2. Key Components of API Monitoring

Effective monitoring involves tracking key aspects of your API's activity to spot any unusual or malicious behavior. Here are the essential components to monitor:

a. Traffic Patterns and Request Volume

One of the first signs of a security incident is unusual traffic patterns. A sudden spike in requests may indicate a DoS attack, while a low number of requests from an unknown IP address could signal an attempt to access the API without authorization.

- **What to monitor:**
  - Request frequency: Look for patterns that are significantly higher than normal.
  - IP address anomalies: Identify requests from suspicious or unfamiliar IP addresses.

- Geographic location: Monitor if users are accessing your API from unexpected countries or regions.

Best Practice:

- Implement rate limiting and track IP addresses that exceed request thresholds to identify potential attacks.

b. Authentication and Authorization Logs

Authentication logs show when a user attempts to access your API, including login attempts, token usage, and whether the authentication was successful. Monitoring these logs helps identify unauthorized access attempts, such as brute-force attacks or credential stuffing.

- **What to monitor:**
  - Unsuccessful login attempts: Identify patterns of failed logins or repeated attempts to brute-force passwords.

- Token expiry or invalidation: Monitor if expired or invalid tokens are used in an attempt to access your API.
- Access control failures: Detect instances where users try to access resources they're not authorized to access.

Best Practice:

- Set up alerts for a high volume of failed login attempts or token validation failures.

c. Error Rates and Response Codes

Unusual error rates can often indicate underlying security problems. For instance, a spike in 5xx (server errors) or 4xx (client errors) could be the result of attempted exploits or misconfigured endpoints. Monitoring error rates helps you identify unusual behavior that could lead to a breach.

- What to monitor:

    - 4xx and 5xx response codes: Track when error codes appear unexpectedly and investigate the root cause.

    - Specific endpoints with high error rates: Focus on endpoints that generate consistent errors, as these could be targeted by attackers.

Best Practice:

- Set thresholds for error rates that trigger automatic alerts to investigate possible attacks or misconfigurations.

3. Tools for API Security Monitoring

There are several tools available to help automate and streamline the process of monitoring API security. These tools provide real-time visibility into your API's health, performance, and security. Below are some of the most effective tools and platforms you can use:

a. Web Application Firewalls (WAFs)

A WAF acts as a barrier between your API and incoming web traffic, filtering malicious requests before they reach your API. Many modern WAFs have built-in API security features such as request rate limiting, signature-based detection, and real-time alerting.

- **Popular WAFs:**
  - **Cloudflare:** Offers DDoS protection, rate limiting, and bot mitigation.
  - **AWS WAF:** Provides security monitoring and real-time logging of API requests.
  - **Imperva:** Offers API security monitoring with advanced anomaly detection.

Best Practice:

- Integrate your WAF with logging and alerting tools to get real-time notifications on suspicious activity.

b. API Management Platforms

API management platforms like Apigee, Kong, and Amazon API Gateway provide centralized monitoring for all your APIs. These platforms often include analytics dashboards that help you track usage, performance, and security incidents.

- Key features:
    - Traffic analytics and visualization
    - Real-time alerting for security breaches
    - Built-in logging for auditing and compliance

Best Practice:

- Use these platforms to gather detailed insights into API usage and identify patterns that may suggest malicious activity.

c. SIEM (Security Information and Event Management) Systems

SIEM platforms such as Splunk, ELK Stack, and Graylog aggregate security data from various sources (e.g., WAFs, API logs, authentication systems) and analyze it to identify potential threats. SIEM tools provide centralized log management, advanced analytics, and automated alerts.

- Key benefits:
  - Correlate data from multiple sources
  - Real-time threat detection and incident response
  - Detailed forensic analysis for post-incident investigations

Best Practice:

- Use SIEM systems to aggregate API logs and gain a unified view of your API security posture.

4. Setting Up Automated Alerts

While continuous monitoring is crucial, it's equally important to have automated alerting in place. Automated alerts help you respond to incidents as soon as they are detected, reducing the time to mitigate threats.

How to Set Up Alerts:

- **Threshold-Based Alerts:** Set specific thresholds (e.g., 100 failed logins in an hour) to trigger alerts when certain events exceed predefined limits.

- **Anomaly Detection:** Use machine learning or rule-based algorithms to detect patterns that deviate from the norm, such as a sudden increase in traffic or failed authentication attempts.

- **Severity Levels:** Classify alerts into different severity levels (e.g., low, medium, high) to prioritize response actions.

Best Practice:

- Test and fine-tune alert thresholds to minimize false positives while ensuring timely responses to real threats.

5. Incident Response and Post-Incident Analysis

When a security incident occurs, it's essential to have a well-defined incident response plan in place. Monitoring tools will help you detect potential incidents early, but having the right processes in place will enable you to act swiftly and mitigate any damage.

Steps to Take During an Incident:

1. **Identify the Source:** Use logs and monitoring data to determine the source of the attack (e.g., specific IP addresses, endpoints).
2. **Contain the Incident:** Immediately block suspicious requests, such as those from a known malicious IP address or source.

3. **Investigate and Remediate:** Investigate the scope of the breach and patch any vulnerabilities that were exploited.

4. **Notify Stakeholders:** If necessary, inform users and relevant authorities about the breach, following applicable regulations like GDPR or CCPA.

Post-Incident Analysis:

- After the incident is contained, conduct a post-mortem analysis to understand what went wrong and how to prevent similar incidents in the future.

- Update your security policies, monitoring tools, and incident response plan based on the lessons learned from the breach

Chapter Nine

Secure API Design and Best Practices for Building

Robust APIs

Designing a secure API requires more than just implementing protective measures after development. A secure API should start with a strong foundation in its design phase, considering both security and scalability as essential components of the API's structure. This chapter will focus on best practices for designing secure APIs, highlighting strategies for minimizing risks, enhancing security, and building APIs that can withstand evolving threats.

By integrating security into the design process from the beginning, you'll avoid costly fixes and vulnerabilities down the road. In this chapter, we'll cover key design principles, practical security practices, and essential steps to follow when building secure APIs.

1. Principles of Secure API Design

When designing an API, several key principles should guide your decisions to ensure it remains secure throughout its lifecycle.

a. Least Privilege Access

One of the foundational principles in API design is the principle of least privilege. This means that an API should only give access to resources and actions that are absolutely necessary for a specific user or service to perform its tasks. Avoid over-provisioning permissions, and ensure that access control is tightly scoped.

- How to apply:
  - Use role-based access control (RBAC) to enforce the principle of least privilege.
  - Define clear user roles and restrict access to sensitive operations only to users who need it.

Best Practice:

- Regularly review and update user permissions to ensure that unnecessary access is revoked, and only essential actions are available to each role.

b. Secure by Design

Security should be an integral part of the design process, not an afterthought. Ensure your API design incorporates security best practices from the very beginning. This includes choosing secure communication protocols, implementing strong authentication methods, and validating input data.

- How to apply:
  - Use HTTPS for all communication, ensuring that data in transit is encrypted.
  - Implement security measures like input validation and sanitization to prevent common attack vectors such as SQL

injection, cross-site scripting (XSS), and cross-site request forgery (CSRF).

Best Practice:

- Conduct a security audit during the design phase to identify potential vulnerabilities before development starts.

c. Modularity and Flexibility

A modular approach to API design allows components to be updated or replaced independently without affecting the overall security and functionality of the API. This approach also makes it easier to implement security fixes and scale your API as needed.

- **How to apply:**
  - Design APIs in a way that allows individual components (e.g., authentication, logging, rate limiting) to be modular.
  - Choose flexible API architectures such as REST or GraphQL that can scale as the API grows.

Best Practice:

- Implement versioning early in the design process to ensure that changes or upgrades to individual modules don't break backward compatibility.

2. Authentication and Authorization Mechanisms

Authentication and authorization are two of the most critical components of API security. Without robust authentication and authorization mechanisms in place, your API is susceptible to unauthorized access, data breaches, and abuse.

a. Strong Authentication

Authentication verifies the identity of a user or service attempting to access the API. The stronger the authentication, the more difficult it will be for attackers to gain unauthorized access.

- **How to apply:**
  - Use OAuth 2.0, OpenID Connect, or API keys for secure and scalable authentication.
  - Implement Multi-Factor Authentication (MFA) wherever possible to add an additional layer of security.

Best Practice:

- Use token-based authentication like JWT (JSON Web Tokens) to manage sessions securely, and set an expiration time on tokens to reduce the risk of abuse.

b. Fine-Grained Authorization

Once a user is authenticated, it's important to ensure that they can only access the resources and actions they're authorized to interact with. This step prevents unauthorized access to sensitive data and ensures users have the appropriate level of access.

- **How to apply:**
  - Implement role-based access control (RBAC) to assign different levels of access based on user roles.
  - For more complex scenarios, consider attribute-based access control (ABAC), which

uses attributes like the user's location or device type to determine access.

Best Practice:

- Regularly audit user roles and permissions to ensure they align with the least privilege principle.

3. Data Protection and Encryption

Data protection is vital in ensuring the confidentiality, integrity, and availability of information transferred through APIs. Proper encryption methods must be used both in transit and at rest to prevent unauthorized access and data breaches.

a. Secure Data in Transit

Encrypting data in transit ensures that sensitive information, such as API keys, passwords, and personal data, is protected from eavesdropping, man-in-the-middle attacks, and tampering.

- **How to apply:**
  - Always use HTTPS (SSL/TLS) to secure communication between clients and servers.
  - Use strong encryption algorithms like AES-256 for additional data protection.

Best Practice:

- Regularly update your SSL/TLS certificates to ensure secure communication.

b. Secure Data at Rest

Encrypting sensitive data at rest ensures that even if an attacker gains access to your server, they cannot read or alter the data without proper decryption keys.

- **How to apply:**
  - Use file system encryption, database encryption, or encrypt sensitive data using tools like AWS KMS (Key Management Service).
  - Store encryption keys securely, separate from the encrypted data.

Best Practice:

- Implement regular audits and key rotation policies to ensure encryption keys remain secure and properly managed.

4. Input Validation and Data Sanitization

One of the most common attack vectors for APIs is input manipulation. Without proper input validation and data sanitization, your API is vulnerable to attacks such as SQL injection, XSS, and other forms of data manipulation.

a. Validate All Inputs

All data coming into your API from users or external services should be treated as untrusted. Validate inputs against a strict schema to ensure that only valid data is processed.

- How to apply:
  - Use input validation libraries to ensure data adheres to expected formats.
  - Define and enforce strict validation rules for every API endpoint.

Best Practice:

- Never trust user input. Always sanitize data before storing or processing it.

b. Sanitize User-Generated Content

If your API allows users to submit content (such as comments or form submissions), ensure that the content is sanitized to prevent malicious code from being executed.

- How to apply:
  - Use libraries or frameworks to escape user input before rendering it on the client-side to prevent XSS attacks.
  - Ensure any file uploads are scanned for malware before processing.

Best Practice:

- Limit the types of files that users can upload (e.g., only allow image files) and scan uploads for any malicious content.

5. Rate Limiting and Throttling

Rate limiting is a fundamental technique used to protect APIs from abuse, such as denial-of-service (DoS) attacks and brute-force attempts. By controlling the number of requests a user can make in a given time frame, you can prevent malicious actors from overwhelming your API with excessive traffic.

How to apply:

- Set rate limits per user, IP address, or service.
- Implement dynamic throttling to adjust limits based on traffic patterns.

Best Practice:

- Use third-party services, such as API gateways (e.g., Kong, AWS API Gateway), to enforce rate limiting and throttling efficiently.

6. Continuous Security Testing and Audits

API security should not be a one-time consideration. Regular security testing and audits are crucial for identifying vulnerabilities and ensuring that your API remains secure over time.

a. Penetration Testing

Penetration testing simulates attacks on your API to identify vulnerabilities that could be exploited. It's a proactive way to find security gaps before real attackers do.

- How to apply:
  - Regularly conduct penetration tests on your API using both automated tools and manual techniques.
  - Engage external security experts for unbiased testing and thorough analysis.

Best Practice:

- Schedule penetration tests on a quarterly basis or after significant changes to the API.

b. Security Audits and Monitoring

Regular security audits and continuous monitoring are key to keeping your API secure in the long run. Ensure that logging and monitoring systems are in place to track the health and security status of your API.

- **How to apply:**
    - Review API access logs regularly to detect unusual activity.
    - Monitor for signs of potential threats, such as rapid changes in traffic volume or unusual authentication requests.

Best Practice:

- Use SIEM systems to aggregate logs and detect patterns of suspicious behavior.

Chapter Ten

Managing API Versions and Ensuring Backward Compatibility

As your API evolves, you will likely need to introduce new features, fix bugs, and implement security updates. However, making these changes without disrupting existing clients or breaking backward compatibility can be challenging. This chapter focuses on the importance of managing API versions and maintaining backward compatibility to ensure that your users experience minimal disruption while benefiting from new functionality and improvements.

API versioning allows you to make changes to your API while still supporting older versions for clients who may rely on them. By managing versions carefully, you can strike a balance between innovation and stability, making it easier for clients to adopt new versions of the API when they are ready.

In this chapter, we will explore various versioning strategies, best practices for maintaining backward compatibility, and how to handle deprecations effectively.

1. Why API Versioning Matters

API versioning is essential because it enables you to make updates to your API without breaking existing integrations. Without versioning, changes such as altering response formats, removing features, or modifying endpoint behavior could cause significant issues for clients that depend on the current version of the API.

Key Benefits of API Versioning:

- **Non-Disruptive Changes:** Versioning allows you to introduce changes to your API while keeping older versions available for clients who need time to transition.
- **Security Updates:** Security vulnerabilities can be addressed in new versions without impacting users who are still using older versions.
- **Long-Term Support:** Clients can continue using older versions without immediate pressure to upgrade, allowing them to adopt new versions at their own pace.

2. Versioning Strategies

There are several strategies for API versioning, each with its own pros and cons. The versioning strategy you choose should align with the goals of your API and the needs of your users.

a. URI Versioning (Path Versioning)

In this approach, the API version is included as part of the URL path. This is one of the most common and straightforward methods of versioning.

Example:

bash

```
https://api.example.com/v1/users
https://api.example.com/v2/users
```

Pros:

- Simple and easy to implement.
- Clearly indicates which version of the API is being used.
- Makes it easy to separate different versions of the API.

Cons:

- URL paths can become cluttered with multiple versions if not managed properly.
- Can lead to redundant API definitions for each version, making maintenance harder.

Best Practice:

- Use a clear and consistent versioning format (e.g., /v1/ or /v2/) and document version changes carefully.

b. Query Parameter Versioning

In this method, the API version is specified as a query parameter in the URL. This allows you to keep the same endpoint and pass the version number as part of the request.

Example:

arduino

```
https://api.example.com/users?version=1
https://api.example.com/users?version=2
```

Pros:

- Keeps URLs clean and reduces clutter.
- Allows for versioning without changing the base URL structure.

Cons:

- Less obvious to the user than URI versioning.
- Can lead to inconsistency if multiple query parameters are used.

Best Practice:

- Ensure that query parameters are clearly defined in your API documentation.

c. Header Versioning

In this approach, the version is specified in the HTTP request headers, often using a custom header.

Example:

bash

```
GET /users
Headers:
  Accept: application/vnd.example.v1+json
```

Pros:

- Keeps URLs clean and avoids clutter.
- Allows clients to request specific versions without changing the base endpoint or query parameters.

Cons:

- Slightly more complex to implement.
- Requires clients to configure headers correctly.

Best Practice:

- Use the `Accept` header with custom media types for versioning (e.g., `application/vnd.example.v1+json`).

d. Accept Header Versioning (Content Negotiation)

Content negotiation is a powerful method of API versioning. The API determines which version to respond with based on the `Accept` header in the request. This can be useful for APIs that serve multiple formats or versions of content.

Example:

bash

```
GET /users
Accept: application/vnd.example.v1+json
```

Pros:

- Very clean URL structure.
- Enables multiple versions and formats without altering the endpoint.

Cons:

- More complex to implement.
- Requires understanding of content negotiation by the client.

3. Best Practices for Maintaining Backward Compatibility

Ensuring backward compatibility is crucial when making changes to an API. Here are some strategies to minimize disruption and maintain compatibility for clients using older versions:

a. Deprecation Policy

When you need to remove or change a feature, it's important to communicate these changes clearly to your users. A deprecation policy allows clients to prepare for upcoming changes by notifying them in advance and giving them time to adapt.

How to apply:

- Mark deprecated features in your API documentation.
- Provide clear versioning notes indicating when a feature will be removed.
- Implement a transition period where deprecated features are still supported.

Best Practice:

- Set a clear timeline for deprecation (e.g., a few months to a year) and notify clients regularly about the deprecation status.

b. Non-Breaking Changes First

When making changes to your API, always aim to make non-breaking changes first. These changes should not affect existing functionality and should enhance or extend the capabilities of the API.

Examples of non-breaking changes include:

- Adding new fields to API responses.
- Introducing new optional query parameters.
- Extending support for additional formats or protocols.

Best Practice:

- Ensure that any changes you make do not break existing client integrations unless absolutely necessary.

c. Backward-Compatible Changes

When introducing breaking changes (e.g., removing an endpoint or changing data formats), you must carefully manage these changes to ensure backward compatibility. One common approach is to introduce new API versions alongside the existing one, allowing users to gradually transition.

How to apply:

- Add new features or endpoints in a new version while keeping the old versions functional.
- Clearly document the differences between versions and help clients migrate smoothly.

Best Practice:

- Provide migration guides for clients, explaining the differences between versions and how to transition without disruptions.

4. Handling Deprecated Endpoints

As your API evolves, some endpoints may become obsolete and need to be removed. To prevent issues, you must manage deprecated endpoints carefully.

a. Clear Deprecation Notices

When an endpoint is marked for deprecation, ensure that users are aware of the change before it is removed.

How to apply:

- Send API response headers or messages indicating that an endpoint is deprecated.
- Provide details on the deprecation in the API documentation.

Best Practice:

- Offer a grace period during which both the old and new versions are available.

b. Versioning of Deprecation Messages

If an endpoint or feature is deprecated, version the deprecation messages to ensure that clients using the old version are informed properly.

How to apply:

- Include deprecation warnings in response headers or response bodies.
- Include detailed information on the removal timeline and alternatives.

5. Migrating Between API Versions

When it's time to transition clients from one version of the API to another, a smooth migration strategy is necessary.

a. API Migrations: Gradual Transition

Migrations should be gradual, allowing clients to adapt to new versions at their own pace. Instead of abruptly discontinuing old versions, offer a coexisting period where both versions are available.

How to apply:

- Offer a well-defined transition period where both old and new versions are operational.
- Provide clear upgrade paths, including detailed changelogs and migration guides.

Best Practice:

- Offer tools and automation options to assist clients in migrating to the latest version of your API.

6. Versioning and Documentation

API versioning must be well-documented to ensure users understand which version they are using and how to transition between versions. This includes clearly indicating the supported versions, version history, and deprecation timelines in your documentation.

How to apply:

- Include a version history section in the API documentation.
- Provide a migration guide that explains changes between versions and offers steps for transitioning smoothly.

Best Practice:

- Regularly update your API documentation to reflect the most recent changes and versions.

Chapter Eleven

Monitoring, Logging, and Auditing API Activity

Monitoring, logging, and auditing are critical components of API security, performance optimization, and troubleshooting. Without an effective monitoring and logging strategy, it becomes nearly impossible to detect security breaches, identify performance bottlenecks, or understand how your API is being used. In this chapter, we will explore the importance of monitoring API activity, logging key events, and auditing user actions to ensure that your API remains secure, performant, and reliable.

We will also cover best practices for setting up logging systems, analyzing logs, and using the collected data to improve both API security and user experience.

1. Importance of Monitoring and Logging

Monitoring and logging are two distinct but complementary activities that are vital to the successful operation of an API. Monitoring refers to tracking the health and performance of the API in real-time, while logging involves capturing detailed records of API requests, responses, and system events.

Why Monitoring and Logging Matter:

- **Security Monitoring:** Detecting suspicious activity or potential security breaches early is key to mitigating threats. Monitoring helps track unusual usage patterns or unauthorized access attempts.

- **Performance Optimization:** Monitoring system resources (e.g., CPU, memory usage, and response times) allows you to optimize the API's performance and avoid downtime.
- **Debugging and Troubleshooting:** Logs provide a detailed account of what happened during an API call, which is invaluable for diagnosing issues or bugs.
- **Auditing and Compliance:** For APIs dealing with sensitive or regulated data, maintaining detailed audit logs is necessary for compliance with standards and regulations such as GDPR or HIPAA.

2. Setting Up API Monitoring

Effective monitoring provides you with real-time visibility into the performance and health of your API, allowing you to detect issues and address them proactively.

a. Key Metrics to Monitor

To ensure the smooth operation of your API, you should monitor the following key metrics:

1. **Response Time:** Measure the time it takes for your API to respond to a request. This is a critical performance metric and should be monitored for each endpoint.
2. **Error Rate:** Track the number and types of errors (e.g., 4xx and 5xx status codes) occurring in the system. A sudden spike in error rates may indicate a bug or failure.
3. **Throughput (Requests per Second):** Monitor how many requests your API is handling in a given

period to understand traffic patterns and plan for scaling.

4. **Latency:** Measure the time delay in processing requests. High latency can negatively impact the user experience.

5. **Uptime/Downtime:** Track whether your API is available or down. Prolonged downtime can significantly affect users and result in business losses.

6. **Resource Usage (CPU, Memory, Disk I/O):** These metrics provide insights into the infrastructure and help identify performance bottlenecks or resource exhaustion.

7. **Traffic Volume by Endpoint:** Analyze traffic patterns by endpoint to identify which parts of your API are being used the most and may require optimization.

b. Tools for API Monitoring

To effectively monitor your API, you can use third-party monitoring tools that provide real-time dashboards and alerting systems.

Popular Monitoring Tools:

- **Prometheus & Grafana:** Open-source tools for monitoring and alerting, widely used for collecting and visualizing API performance metrics.
- **New Relic:** A cloud-based tool that provides real-time insights into API performance, user interactions, and infrastructure health.
- **Datadog:** Offers comprehensive monitoring for API performance, including error tracking and resource usage analysis.

- **AWS CloudWatch:** Amazon's native monitoring tool that tracks API performance and infrastructure metrics in AWS environments.

3. Implementing API Logging

While monitoring focuses on real-time performance, logging captures the detailed history of every API request and response. Proper logging is essential for troubleshooting, identifying trends, and ensuring security.

a. What to Log

When logging API activity, it's crucial to capture relevant information while maintaining privacy and compliance.

Key Log Information:

1. **Request Details:**
   - Timestamp: Record the exact time of the request.
   - Request Method: GET, POST, PUT, DELETE, etc.
   - Request URL/Path: The endpoint that was hit.
   - Headers: Information about the request headers (e.g., authorization token, content type).
   - Query Parameters: Any query parameters or body data submitted with the request.
2. **Response Details:**
   - Status Code: The HTTP status code (e.g., 200 OK, 404 Not Found, 500 Internal Server Error).
   - Response Body: Record the response body, especially in the case of errors.

- Response Time: The time taken to process the request.
- Error Messages: Any error messages or exceptions encountered during the request.

3. **User Details (if applicable):**
   - User ID or IP address: Identifying information for the user making the request (ensure privacy and compliance with laws like GDPR).

4. **System Events:**
   - Server health events (e.g., crashes, outages).
   - Resource utilization spikes (e.g., CPU, memory).

b. Log Format and Storage

Logs should be structured in a consistent and machine-readable format to allow for easy parsing and analysis. A common log format is JSON, which is lightweight and easy to process.

Log Storage Considerations:

- Store logs in a central location for easy access and analysis.
- Use cloud-based log storage services like **AWS CloudWatch Logs**, **Elasticsearch**, or **Google Cloud Logging**.
- For sensitive data, ensure that logs are stored securely and that access is restricted.

c. Log Retention and Rotation

Logs can accumulate quickly, and it's important to manage their retention effectively to avoid unnecessary storage costs and ensure that only useful data is kept.

Log Retention Best Practices:

- Set a retention period based on business needs (e.g., 30 days for regular logs, 1 year for audit logs).
- Implement log rotation to avoid filling up disk space.

4. API Auditing for Security and Compliance

Auditing allows you to track and review the activities performed by users, administrators, and services interacting with your API. This is particularly important for APIs handling sensitive data or complying with regulations such as HIPAA or GDPR.

a. What to Audit

In addition to general logging, you should consider auditing the following actions:

- **User Authentication and Authorization:** Track successful and failed login attempts, token generation, and role changes.
- **Access to Sensitive Data:** Log when sensitive data (e.g., personal information or financial data) is accessed, modified, or deleted.
- **Changes to API Permissions:** Track changes to user roles, API keys, and permissions.
- **Admin Actions:** Record administrative actions such as configuration changes, API key rotations, and access to restricted areas of the API.

b. Compliance Considerations

For APIs handling sensitive or regulated data, it's crucial to maintain an audit trail that meets legal and regulatory standards. You should ensure that:

- Logs are immutable and cannot be tampered with.
- Audit logs are stored in a secure, encrypted location.
- Logs are accessible only to authorized personnel.
- The data is retained for the required period as specified by regulatory requirements.

5. Analyzing Logs for Insights

Once you have set up logging, the next step is to analyze the data to uncover insights that can improve your API's performance, security, and user experience.

a. Troubleshooting and Debugging

Logs can be invaluable when troubleshooting issues. By reviewing logs, you can pinpoint the root cause of issues such as:

- **API Errors:** Find the exact error message and determine which part of the request caused it.
- **Performance Bottlenecks:** Identify which endpoints or operations are taking longer than expected and need optimization.
- **Unauthorized Access:** Detect suspicious access patterns, such as unusual IP addresses or failed login attempts.

b. Identifying Usage Patterns

By analyzing API traffic logs, you can discover trends that help you understand user behavior and plan future improvements:

- Which endpoints are most frequently accessed?
- What time of day does traffic peak?

- Are there any patterns of failed requests or errors?

6. Using Monitoring and Logging Data to Improve API Security

By continuously monitoring and logging API activity, you can identify security threats and implement proactive measures. Some common security threats that can be detected through monitoring and logging include:

- **DDoS Attacks:** Monitoring traffic volume can help identify potential Distributed Denial of Service (DDoS) attacks.
- **Brute Force Attacks:** Monitoring login attempts can help detect brute force attacks trying to guess user credentials.
- **SQL Injection Attempts:** Logs that capture request data can help identify suspicious patterns indicative of SQL injection.

Monitoring, logging, and auditing are critical components of API security, performance optimization, and troubleshooting. Without an effective monitoring and logging strategy, it becomes nearly impossible to detect security breaches, identify performance bottlenecks, or understand how your API is being used. In this chapter, we will explore the importance of monitoring API activity, logging key events, and auditing user actions to ensure that your API remains secure, performant, and reliable.

We will also cover best practices for setting up logging systems, analyzing logs, and using the collected data to improve both API security and user experience.

1. Importance of Monitoring and Logging

Monitoring and logging are two distinct but complementary activities that are vital to the successful operation of an API. Monitoring refers to tracking the health and performance of the API in real-time, while logging involves capturing detailed records of API requests, responses, and system events.

Why Monitoring and Logging Matter:

- Security Monitoring: Detecting suspicious activity or potential security breaches early is key to mitigating threats. Monitoring helps track unusual usage patterns or unauthorized access attempts.

- Performance Optimization: Monitoring system resources (e.g., CPU, memory usage, and response times) allows you to optimize the API's performance and avoid downtime.

- Debugging and Troubleshooting: Logs provide a detailed account of what happened during an API call, which is invaluable for diagnosing issues or bugs.

- Auditing and Compliance: For APIs dealing with sensitive or regulated data, maintaining detailed audit logs is necessary for compliance with standards and regulations such as GDPR or HIPAA.

2. Setting Up API Monitoring

Effective monitoring provides you with real-time visibility into the performance and health of your API, allowing you to detect issues and address them proactively.

a. Key Metrics to Monitor

To ensure the smooth operation of your API, you should monitor the following key metrics:

1. Response Time: Measure the time it takes for your API to respond to a request. This is a critical performance metric and should be monitored for each endpoint.

2. Error Rate: Track the number and types of errors (e.g., 4xx and 5xx status codes) occurring in the system. A sudden spike in error rates may indicate a bug or failure.

3. Throughput (Requests per Second): Monitor how many requests your API is handling in a given period to understand traffic patterns and plan for scaling.

4. Latency: Measure the time delay in processing requests. High latency can negatively impact the user experience.

5. Uptime/Downtime: Track whether your API is available or down. Prolonged downtime can significantly affect users and result in business losses.

6. Resource Usage (CPU, Memory, Disk I/O): These metrics provide insights into the infrastructure and help identify performance bottlenecks or resource exhaustion.

7. Traffic Volume by Endpoint: Analyze traffic patterns by endpoint to identify which parts of your API are being used the most and may require optimization.

b. Tools for API Monitoring

To effectively monitor your API, you can use third-party monitoring tools that provide real-time dashboards and alerting systems.

Popular Monitoring Tools:

- Prometheus & Grafana: Open-source tools for monitoring and alerting, widely used for collecting and visualizing API performance metrics.

- New Relic: A cloud-based tool that provides real-time insights into API performance, user interactions, and infrastructure health.

- Datadog: Offers comprehensive monitoring for API performance, including error tracking and resource usage analysis.

- AWS CloudWatch: Amazon's native monitoring tool that tracks API performance and infrastructure metrics in AWS environments.

3. Implementing API Logging

While monitoring focuses on real-time performance, logging captures the detailed history of every API request and response. Proper logging is essential for troubleshooting, identifying trends, and ensuring security.

a. What to Log

When logging API activity, it's crucial to capture relevant information while maintaining privacy and compliance.

Key Log Information:

1. Request Details:
   - Timestamp: Record the exact time of the request.

- Request Method: GET, POST, PUT, DELETE, etc.

- Request URL/Path: The endpoint that was hit.

- Headers: Information about the request headers (e.g., authorization token, content type).

- Query Parameters: Any query parameters or body data submitted with the request.

2. Response Details:

- Status Code: The HTTP status code (e.g., 200 OK, 404 Not Found, 500 Internal Server Error).

- Response Body: Record the response body, especially in the case of errors.

- Response Time: The time taken to process the request.

- Error Messages: Any error messages or exceptions encountered during the request.

3. User Details (if applicable):

- User ID or IP address: Identifying information for the user making the request (ensure privacy and compliance with laws like GDPR).

4. System Events:
   - Server health events (e.g., crashes, outages).
   - Resource utilization spikes (e.g., CPU, memory).

b. Log Format and Storage

Logs should be structured in a consistent and machine-readable format to allow for easy parsing and analysis. A common log format is JSON, which is lightweight and easy to process.

Log Storage Considerations:

- Store logs in a central location for easy access and analysis.
- Use cloud-based log storage services like AWS CloudWatch Logs, Elasticsearch, or Google Cloud Logging.

- For sensitive data, ensure that logs are stored securely and that access is restricted.

c. Log Retention and Rotation

Logs can accumulate quickly, and it's important to manage their retention effectively to avoid unnecessary storage costs and ensure that only useful data is kept.

Log Retention Best Practices:

- Set a retention period based on business needs (e.g., 30 days for regular logs, 1 year for audit logs).
- Implement log rotation to avoid filling up disk space.

4. API Auditing for Security and Compliance

Auditing allows you to track and review the activities performed by users, administrators, and services interacting with your API. This is particularly important for APIs handling sensitive data or complying with regulations such as HIPAA or GDPR.

a. What to Audit

In addition to general logging, you should consider auditing the following actions:

- User Authentication and Authorization: Track successful and failed login attempts, token generation, and role changes.
- Access to Sensitive Data: Log when sensitive data (e.g., personal information or financial data) is accessed, modified, or deleted.
- Changes to API Permissions: Track changes to user roles, API keys, and permissions.
- Admin Actions: Record administrative actions such as configuration changes, API key rotations, and access to restricted areas of the API.

b. Compliance Considerations

For APIs handling sensitive or regulated data, it's crucial to maintain an audit trail that meets legal and regulatory standards. You should ensure that:

- Logs are immutable and cannot be tampered with.
- Audit logs are stored in a secure, encrypted location.
- Logs are accessible only to authorized personnel.
- The data is retained for the required period as specified by regulatory requirements.

5. Analyzing Logs for Insights

Once you have set up logging, the next step is to analyze the data to uncover insights that can improve your API's performance, security, and user experience.

a. Troubleshooting and Debugging

Logs can be invaluable when troubleshooting issues. By reviewing logs, you can pinpoint the root cause of issues such as:

- API Errors: Find the exact error message and determine which part of the request caused it.
- Performance Bottlenecks: Identify which endpoints or operations are taking longer than expected and need optimization.
- Unauthorized Access: Detect suspicious access patterns, such as unusual IP addresses or failed login attempts.

b. Identifying Usage Patterns

By analyzing API traffic logs, you can discover trends that help you understand user behavior and plan future improvements:

- Which endpoints are most frequently accessed?
- What time of day does traffic peak?
- Are there any patterns of failed requests or errors?

6. Using Monitoring and Logging Data to Improve API Security

By continuously monitoring and logging API activity, you can identify security threats and implement proactive measures. Some common security threats that can be detected through monitoring and logging include:

- DDoS Attacks: Monitoring traffic volume can help identify potential Distributed Denial of Service (DDoS) attacks.

- Brute Force Attacks: Monitoring login attempts can help detect brute force attacks trying to guess user credentials.

- SQL Injection Attempts: Logs that capture request data can help identify suspicious patterns indicative of SQL injection.

Chapter Twelve

Emerging Trends and Best Practices

API security is a dynamic and ever-evolving field. As technology continues to advance, so do the methods and threats associated with securing web and mobile application programming interfaces. In this final chapter, we will explore emerging trends in API security, the latest best practices, and how to stay ahead of evolving threats.

Understanding future developments and preparing your APIs for emerging security challenges will help you stay resilient against attacks and continue to deliver secure, high-performing services.

1. The Evolution of API Security

API security has come a long way from its early days, when it was mostly about securing basic authentication and protecting data in transit. As the digital landscape evolves, so do the threats that target APIs. Today, APIs are often at the heart of modern applications, making them more attractive targets for attackers.

Key Trends in API Security:

- **Microservices and API Gateways:** The rise of microservices architecture and the increased adoption of API gateways are shifting the way APIs are managed and secured. With microservices, APIs are often exposed between independent services, creating multiple attack vectors. API gateways are now crucial for managing authentication, routing, and rate limiting to ensure secure API communication.

- **Serverless Architectures:** Serverless computing reduces the overhead of managing servers, but it also introduces new security concerns, such as ensuring that functions within serverless environments are secure. Since serverless functions often have access to other services via APIs, securing these interactions is a top priority.

- **AI and Machine Learning in Security:** Artificial Intelligence (AI) and Machine Learning (ML) are being integrated into API security to predict, detect, and mitigate security threats in real-time. For instance, anomaly detection algorithms powered by machine learning can identify patterns of abnormal API behavior, flagging them for further investigation.

- **Zero Trust Security Model:** The Zero Trust model operates on the principle that no user or system, inside or outside the network, should be trusted by default. This approach is gaining popularity for securing APIs by ensuring that every access request is verified, even from users within the internal network.

2. Securing APIs in the Era of Cloud-Native Applications

With the growing shift towards cloud-native applications, API security has become more complex. APIs are now exposed across multiple services and environments, requiring advanced security measures to ensure that they remain protected.

a. Cloud-Based API Security Best Practices:

1. **Use Cloud-Native API Security Tools:** Major cloud providers (AWS, Azure, Google Cloud) offer tools to protect APIs, such as API firewalls, DDoS protection, and threat intelligence services.

2. **Encrypt Data in Transit and at Rest:** Always use encryption (such as TLS/SSL) for data in transit and encrypt sensitive data at rest to prevent data breaches.

3. **Implement Role-Based Access Control (RBAC):** Cloud environments should enforce granular access control policies to ensure that users only have access to the APIs and resources necessary for their role.

4. **API Rate Limiting and Throttling:** Protect APIs from abuse by implementing rate limiting and throttling to control the number of requests per user or IP address.

3. The Role of Automated Security Testing and CI/CD Pipelines

As API development becomes more agile, the need for continuous security testing has grown. APIs are often deployed rapidly in continuous integration/continuous deployment (CI/CD) pipelines, making it crucial to integrate automated security checks throughout the development lifecycle.

a. Benefits of Automated Security Testing:

- Faster Detection of Vulnerabilities: Automated tools can detect common vulnerabilities (e.g., SQL injections, cross-site scripting) early in the development process, reducing the time to identify and fix security issues.

- **Consistency and Coverage**: Automated security tests provide a consistent, repeatable process, ensuring that all components of your API are tested for security flaws.

- **Scalability:** As APIs grow in complexity, it becomes difficult to manually test every endpoint. Automation scales well to handle the growing number of APIs in large environments.

b. Popular Tools for API Security Testing:

- OWASP ZAP (Zed Attack Proxy): An open-source security tool designed for finding vulnerabilities in web applications and APIs.
- **Burp Suite:** A popular web vulnerability scanner that also supports API testing.
- **Postman:** While Postman is primarily used for API testing, it also allows users to create automated API security tests.

4. API Security for the IoT (Internet of Things)

The Internet of Things (IoT) is another area where API security is critical. IoT devices rely heavily on APIs to communicate with each other and with cloud-based services, and securing these APIs is a unique challenge due to the resource limitations of many IoT devices.

Challenges in IoT API Security:

- **Device Vulnerabilities:** Many IoT devices have limited processing power and may not support advanced security features. As a result, API security for IoT must ensure that devices are protected despite these constraints.

- **Insecure API Endpoints:** Since many IoT devices send sensitive data, such as health information or location data, ensuring the security of these APIs is critical.

- **Scalability:** The number of IoT devices is growing rapidly, creating a challenge in managing and securing the vast number of APIs that connect them.

IoT API Security Best Practices:

1. Use Lightweight Cryptography: When dealing with resource-constrained devices, use lightweight cryptographic protocols (e.g., ECC) to secure communications without overburdening the device's resources.

2. **Segregate IoT Networks:** Isolate IoT devices from the core business network to minimize the impact of any potential breaches.

3. **Use Device Authentication:** Ensure each IoT device is securely authenticated before it can access API endpoints, using certificates, API keys, or token-based systems.

4. **Regular Software Updates:** Ensure that IoT devices are regularly updated with security patches, and monitor them for new vulnerabilities.

5. API Security in a Multi-Cloud Environment

With businesses increasingly adopting multi-cloud strategies, APIs often need to interact across different cloud providers and on-premise systems. This introduces additional complexity in securing these cross-cloud interactions.

Best Practices for Multi-Cloud API Security:

- Unified Security Policies: Ensure consistent security policies across all cloud environments to maintain uniform protection levels for APIs.

- Cloud-Native Security Services: Leverage the security tools provided by each cloud provider, but ensure they are integrated and work together seamlessly.

- API Gateway and Service Mesh: Utilize an API gateway or service mesh to manage and secure inter-cloud API communication, including authentication, authorization, and traffic management.

- **Cross-Cloud Threat Detection**: Use centralized threat detection tools that can monitor API activity across multiple cloud environments.

6. Staying Ahead of Emerging Threats

As cyber threats continue to evolve, staying ahead of attackers is crucial. In the future, we can expect to see new attack vectors targeting APIs, including AI-driven attacks, and more sophisticated data manipulation and injection techniques.

Key Measures to Stay Ahead of Threats:

- AI-Powered Threat Intelligence: Leverage machine learning and AI to detect anomalies in API traffic and identify emerging threats before they cause damage.
- **Security Automation**: Automate responses to certain types of attacks, such as rate limiting or blocking IPs associated with brute force attacks, to mitigate damage in real-time.

- **Zero-Day Vulnerability Detection:** Stay proactive in identifying and patching zero-day vulnerabilities in your APIs before they can be exploited by attackers.